ONE YEAR OF AGILE QUOTES

One Year of Agile Quotes

Weekly Mindset Messages

Kelly Brogdon Geyer

Copyright © 2020 by Kelly Brogdon Geyer
All rights reserved. This book or any portion thereof may not be reproduced or used in any many whatsoever without the express written permission of the publisher except for the use of brief quotations in a book review.

ISBN-13: 9798644209026

Dedication

For Markus, my husband, and partner in life. Your encouragement, understanding, tolerance, and affection continuously astonishes me. I am eternally fortunate to be married to my best friend. I love you, Schatzi.

-Your Ladybug

Introduction

While attending San Diego State University, I had a professor who wrote quotes on the whiteboard. I looked forward to coming to class every week because of those little nudges of inspiration. It ignited a spark within me. I began to seek out numerous quotes, sayings, and idioms to fit different occasions. Having fun hobbies makes me happy.

Shortly after I graduated, I became a manager at a bank. I was still quite young and many of my employees were older than me including my assistant. I was looking for ways to inspire my colleagues and also earn their respect as a knowledgeable manager. I remembered my former professor and his quotes. I bought a whiteboard for our breakroom and started to write different quotes each week. Each Monday, I would read the quote during our morning "round up" and ask everyone what it meant for them individually.

It is worth mentioning that the branch where I worked was very diverse. We had employees with different nationalities, ages, genders, marital statuses, family situations, etc. It was easy to visually notice the variances. However, in discussing these quotes, we began to see that we had far more in common than we thought. We had shared values and morals. Our branch began to act as a team with shared goals and the willingness to go above and beyond to help each other.

Many years passed and during my second position as a Scrum Master, I was looking for a way to motivate the organization to keep focused on goals, continuous improvement, collaboration, team building, quality, and any other topics of agility. There was a blog already established so I started posting one quote per week. The discussions that ensued were riveting.

By January 2019, I published my first book *Failing at Agile Transformation: How to Sabotage Your Agile Journey*. I began to think about writing another book. A few people mentioned to me that I should make a book with the quotes I was using for the blog. Initially, I was not really interested. I wanted to make sure any book I published would be helpful for people and serve a purpose. Having the quotes in a blog at work enabled people in the same company to exchange ideas but keeping the quotes confined in the pages of a book would not accomplish what I wanted.

After a short time, I realized that if I wrote a book of quotes, people could use it the same way I used the quotes. They can share with their teams or departments. They can use these magic words as a starting point to wonderful and thought-provoking conversations. If you are reading this now, it means you can use the quotes how you see fit whether you keep them for yourself, use them for inspiration, collaboration, or conversation.

For each, I have provided a quote and then some of my own thoughts about the quote and how it applies to agility. These are only my thoughts so feel free to take the discussion in your own direction and use your interpretation with your teams.

A Year of Agile Quotes

Week 1

"Learn from yesterday, live for today, hope for tomorrow. The important thing is not to stop questioning."
Albert Einstein

This quote from Albert Einstein perfectly captures some of the key principles of Agile. Regularly reflect on the past to find ways to improve. Focus on the present. Keep your goal in mind and make that your priority. Remain hopeful about the future. Continue to cultivate new ideas and never stop questioning why you do things and how you can improve.

Week 2

> "Continuous improvement is better than delayed perfection."
> Mark Twain

Giving up the idea of perfection is difficult for many people. Why? What is the point of trying to be perfect? What does perfect actually mean? Eventually, you have to realize that you are doing your best and that is good enough.

Mark Twain was not an Agile specialist. However, this quote from him accurately describes the mindset most find so difficult to achieve. You do not have to wait until your product is whole and perfect before you present it to your customer. Focus on quality in whatever you deliver. Then continue to make improvements incrementally. Waiting until your product is 100% complete and perfect delays the satisfaction of the customer in having something to touch, feel, and play with.

Week 3

"The world is moving so fast these days that the man who says it can't be done is generally interrupted by someone doing it."

Elbert Hubbard

Every amazing invention in the world had years or even decades preceding it with people thinking the creation was impossible. Think of what life was like before the invention of the wheel, the camera, the telegraph, the light bulb, airplanes, or batteries. Most people alive during these times could not begin to imagine how anyone could build such things.

People usually claim something is not possible for a few reasons. There is a fear of the unknown or fear of failure. You could be facing a lack of creativity or imagination. A person may also simply lack the necessary skills. With focus, determination, knowledge, and hard work, anything is possible. Never allow someone else's self-doubt and personal limitations to prevent you from achieving success.

Week 4

> *"The strength of the team is each individual member. The strength of each member is the team."*
> *Phil Jackson*

Considered one of the greatest basketball coaches of all time, Phil Jackson believed that good teams must have a strong culture, leadership, and good group chemistry. This is true whether you are talking about a sports team, social group, organizational department, or a work team. Being part of a team means helping each other and working as one unit to achieve goals.

A common myth in Agile is that each team member must have the same skills or knowledge that the other team members have. Not only is this untrue, but it could also be detrimental. If you have a team of generalists, then you have a team without any specialists. You do not have anyone who is an expert.

It is more beneficial to have "T-shaped" team members. A T-shaped person is an expert in one area but is also capable

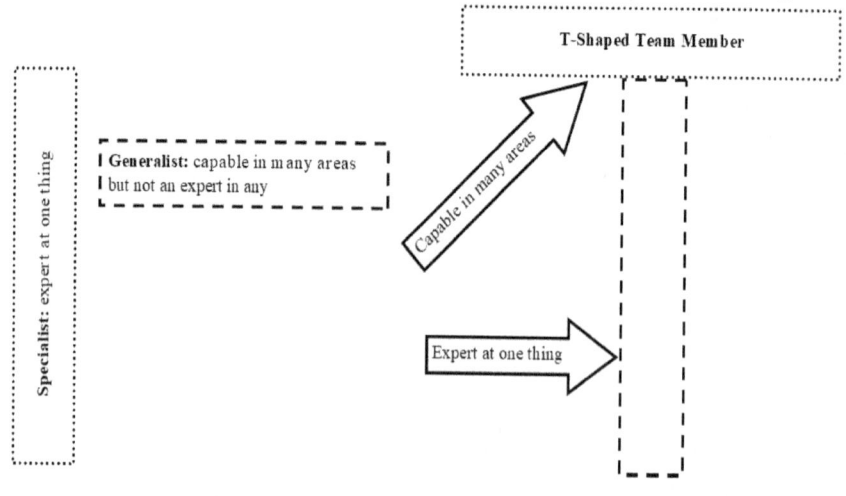

of doing work in other areas. Ideally, you should build a team with people like this. The goal is to have a team that has all the skills and competencies to do the work without requiring help from anyone outside the team.

To make sense of this with a real-world example, think of a human pyramid similar to ones that cheerleaders form with some people on the bottom supporting other people on top. Everyone must have the same basic abilities and skills like balance, flexibility, a certain amount of strength and talent to perform in front of crowds. However, if everyone had the same specialty, the pyramid could never work.

The people on the bottom of the pyramid are usually the strongest and sturdiest because they have to bear the weight of everyone above them. The team members in the middle of the pyramid must have good balance and a strong core. The people at the top of the pyramid are the smallest, weigh the least, and possess aerial skills.

If you had a team with only the people at the bottom, you could not build the pyramid. Likewise, if your team only had members from the middle or top. If your team only possessed the basic skills like the ones mentioned previously, the pyramid would also not be possible. The only way the pyramid is possible is to have a team of T-shaped individuals with some of the same general skills and several different specialties.

Week 5

> *"Service to others is the rent you pay for your room here on earth."*
> *Muhammad Ali*

Muhammad Ali (born Cassius Marcellus Clay Jr.) was an American professional boxer, activist, and philanthropist. His impact on civil rights and peace efforts was insurmountable. Ali focused on practicing his Islamic duty of charity and good deeds, donating millions of dollars to charity organizations and disadvantaged people of all religious backgrounds. His philanthropic work continued despite his failing health until his death in June 2016. Boxing was his job but his acts outside the ring left a lasting legacy worldwide.

As a Scrum Master, you are a servant leader. You support your team by building trust, empowering team members, encouraging them to continuously improve, displaying empathy, staying humble and socially aware. You do not manage the team. They manage themselves. You help remove impediments. You do not solve their problems. You assist the team in solving their own problems. You ensure the team is adhering to the Scrum processes and ceremonies. You do not hide from conflict or problems. You confront issues, not people, head on to come to a resolution.

The role of a Scrum Master is not about making yourself look good or shining a spotlight on your good deeds. It is not even about making your team look good to other people in your organization. Your role is about helping the team function better together by adhering to the Scrum values and principles.

Week 6

"You can't solve a problem with the same mind that created it. First you must change the mind."
Dr. Wayne Dyer

Too often, people underestimate the challenges of adopting one of the Agile frameworks. They mistakenly believe that "becoming Agile" will solve problems within an organization. But becoming Agile isn't simply about having daily meetings, inspecting and adapting, early and continuous delivery, etc. Companies can do all those things and still not be Agile. There is a difference between *being* Agile and just *doing* Agile.

Agile is not a pill that you can take to fix your problems. Agile is a mindset, a philosophy. We have to change the way we think. If we continue to think the same old way while trying to force work in a new way, we will constantly fight a battle within ourselves. We have to change our thinking and then we can attack our problems with fresh eyes and a renewed spirit.

Week 7

> *"When the best leader's work is done the people say, 'We did it ourselves.'"*
> Lao-Tzu

At the heart of Agile are the principles of trust, collaboration, motivation, support, and self-organizing teams. What exactly does self-organization mean? The popular business definition describes a system that functions without outside assistance (Business Dictionary, 2019): "Self-organization...is the ability of a system to spontaneously arrange its components or elements in a purposeful (non-random) manner, under appropriate conditions but without the help of an external agency."

There is usually a tremendous amount of effort, excitement, and new ideas surrounding an Agile transformation. However, you need to take caution when implementing new ideas. You should support individuals and teams to determine how to do their best work instead of enforcing ideas that you think will help them work better. When you *inflict* your "help" rather than offering it, you could be *imposing* your unwelcome ideas on others.

One of the most common pitfalls of an Agile transformation is when organizations continue behaving the same way but mistakenly assume they are changing because they change a few policies or try new things. If you are still inflicting your help and controlling how people do their jobs, you have not changed. Your culture still needs to shift. It is better to support individuals so they can figure out the best way to get their work done.

Week 8

> *"My advice is to stop emphasizing the process frameworks and start focusing on the company culture and mindsets."*
> *Selena Delesie*

Selena Delesie is a Leadership and Transformation Coach, speaker, author, and teacher. She coaches leaders on how to power their vision with soul, connect to their inner voice, and transform every aspect of their life and business.

This quote from her emphasizes what so many companies ignore during an Agile transformation. So focused on daily scrums, backlogs, retrospectives, Kanban boards, etc, they forget about what it means to truly be Agile. Organizations need to reevaluate their existing culture, values, and principles to ensure they morph into the new culture, values, and principles. Analyze the company culture, existing policies, and procedures, environment, hiring practices, etc., and make adjustments accordingly. Focus on people first and that includes employees, customers, building neighbors, contractors, etc. Success will follow because people will feel safe, valued, and happy.

Do not fall victim to focusing on just *doing* Agile things. There is a difference between *doing* Agile and *being* Agile.

Think of it as an iceberg. You only see what is on the surface of the water but there is far more to see underwater. Most organizations begin their Agile journey by focusing most of their efforts on what is above the surface (The Right Set of Tools). Teams are set up, maybe they pay for tools like Jira and Confluence, they purchase physical boards, certain events are set up such as dailies and retrospectives, and coaches are hired to help. Most serious problems will arise from the factors that lie beneath the surface (reward system, culture, structure). There is usually confusion around how to set up goals or objectives, managers are unsure of their new responsibilities and expectations, the hierarchy is disturbed which makes many people nervous, and leaving behind the old command and control style is one of the biggest challenges I have seen firsthand. What can you do to influence the factors below the surface?

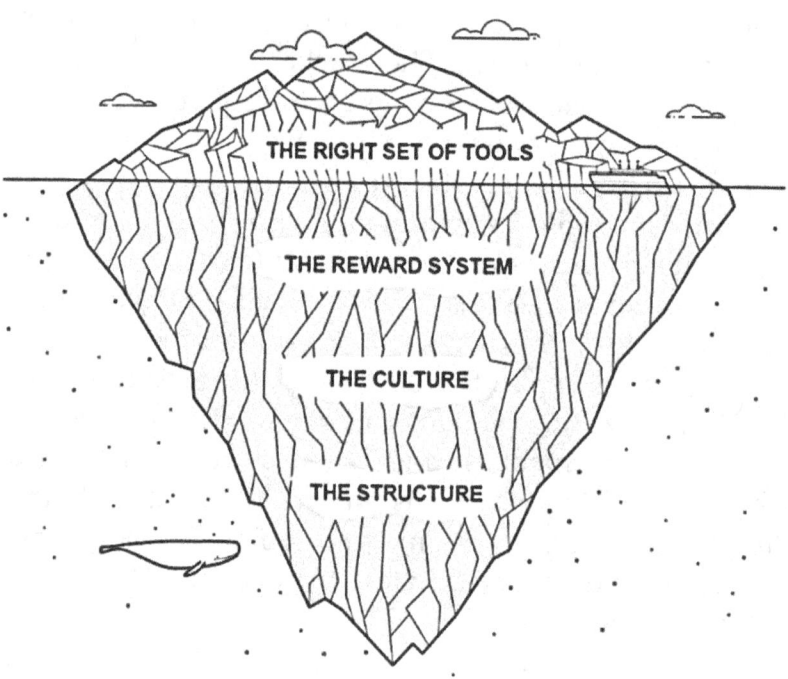

Week 9

"Don't wait until you've reached your goal to be proud of yourself. Be proud of every step you take towards reaching your goal."
Unknown

Any change is difficult. If you want to lose 20 kilograms, it is easy to get discouraged with the scale after you lose 15 kilograms but then the scale refuses to budge. Training to run a marathon is a lofty goal but you could get discouraged if your endurance hits a slump. Agile transformation often leads to similar frustration due to unrealistic expectations of how quickly this change "should" take place.

It is common for teams and individuals within an organization to become frustrated after only a short period during this change. You might hear comments like, "But we aren't Agile *yet*" and "We are still so far from being Agile." While it is important to keep your mind focused on continuous improvement, it is also imperative to reflect on how far you have come already. It is easy to lose sight of this especially because we strive to make incremental improvements rather than large, sweeping changes. Think of it in terms of losing weight. Weight loss is typically slow. It is difficult for the person losing weight to see their progress because they see themselves every day. They may have lost 10 kilos already but still feel discouraged because they do not notice a difference in their appearance. However, if they happen to see someone they have not seen in a few months, that person is likely to notice a big change. This is why most weight loss coaches encourage you to take a "before picture" as a reminder of how far you have come. As an Agile Coach or

Scrum Master, it is important to remind teams of their "before picture." Remind teams of how they worked a year ago and how far they have come. Ask them to think of what they think the next year will bring. Celebrate incremental improvements.

Being Agile is not a destination. You will never be *done*. Being Agile is not about having 100% automated testing or perfect burndown charts. It is about embracing the Agile values and principles and using them as your guide during your periods of reflection. They are the compass directing your decisions. Unlike losing that 20 kilos or running a marathon, being Agile is not a goal that you achieve. It is a mindset to embrace to help you work toward your goals.

Week 10

"It does not matter how slowly you go as long as you do not stop."
Confucius

Everyone realizes that change is difficult. If you are trying to change a habit, it takes an average of two months before a new behavior becomes automatic. In a study conducted in London (Lally, Van Jaarsveld, Potts, & Wardle, 2010), it took anywhere from 18 to 254 days for people to form a new habit depending on the behavior, person, and circumstances. Interestingly, the researchers in this study discovered that "missing one opportunity to perform the behavior did not materially affect the habit formation process." In other words, messing up now and then is okay.

If you are trying to quit smoking, good for you! If you have a moment of weakness and smoke one cigarette while out to dinner with friends, do not beat yourself up over it. Get back on track and do not smoke again. If you are trying to exercise every day for 30 minutes but you missed your workout yesterday, that is not a reason to give up completely. Get back on track and work out today.

Storytime: I have always been slow at running. Always. When I was younger, I was quite athletic but my focus was on swimming so running slow was not a problem. A few years after I had my first son, I decided to start running with a friend of mine. Wow! I was out of shape. I decided that I wanted to be able to run 5 kilometers. We started challenging ourselves by participating in 5k races. Our first one was so much fun and it was a celebratory run for St. Patrick's Day. My second race was uneventful but fun. Although these were "races," they were really just large groups of people who ran or jogged or walked. My slow pace was not noticeable because there were men and women with strollers, kids and elderly people walking, etc.

For my third race, I decided to run a local trail race in my town for Earth Day. I showed up for race day and was shocked. Contrary to the other 2 races with several hundred people, this race had less than 100 participants and they all appeared to be professional athletes! Apparently, almost every participant was a member of the local university Track & Field team along with his or her coaches and I was an out of shape mom who was almost 30 years old! At this point, I realize a trail race means we will run on an actual wooded trail instead of the street like the other races!

I had a choice. I could either leave the race and go home or just try my best even though I am quite clumsy and was nervous about running on an uneven surface. I stayed and ran the race. Halfway through the 5k, I tripped over an exposed tree root and fell into the mud. I thought again about quitting. I could just take my race number off my shirt and pretend like I am just a regular hiker in the woods until I wander back to my car. I did not do that. I wiped the mud off my knees as best as I could and kept trying to run. I was only about 3/4 of the way through the race when everyone else had finished. The race announcer was calling out the names of runners as they crossed the finish line. I had to cross a huge open field to finish. As I came out of the woods and into the field, my head was low. I was so embarrassed.

The announcer called my name. Everyone turned around because they assumed all participants were done. They all stopped drinking their water and eating their fruits. Everyone started clapping and cheering for...me! I learned some important lessons that day besides realizing the amazing positive spirit of absolute strangers. I learned that my choice mattered. I could have gone home before the race started and I would have felt defeated. I chose to keep going even though

A Year of Agile Quotes

I knew before I even started that I would be the slowest person on the trail that day. Quitting would not get me closer to my goal of running an entire 5k. My goal was never about speed. It was about distance.

As you navigate your Agile transformation, this is an important lesson to keep in mind. Each organization, team, and individual works at their own pace. Accept that this transformation will happen at its own pace. Quitting should not be an option. The goal should never be about being fast at Agile transformation. The goal is to improve the customer experience through early and continuous delivery by working collaboratively and focusing on quality while maintaining a sustainable pace. Do not stop. There will be setbacks and you have to keep moving forward. Unlike running a 5k, Agile transformation has no end. You do not run to the finish line. You wake up each day and do the best you can because there is no finish line.

Week 11

> *"The secret to success is good leadership, and good leadership is all about making the lives of your team members or workers better."*
> **Tony Dungy**

Leadership is not the same as management but they do not have to be mutually exclusive. In my personal experience, I have worked with good managers who were not necessarily good leaders and I have worked with inspiring leaders who were not managers. However, when an organization has relied heavily on a command and control management style, proceeding with an Agile transformation will be even more challenging unless that is addressed. A manager will be very uncomfortable with Agile if he or she is accustomed to micromanaging. He or she may even try various tactics to ensure the transformation fails. This is a prime example of a cultural change that needs to happen for the transformation to be successful.

There is a very simple way to start. Managers still need to communicate what they need from their employees. Clearly explain the expectations and objectives and ask what you can do to support them. Give them what they need to get the job done. This may involve ordering a larger computer monitor, a faster server, better lighting in the office, a more comfortable chair, more training in computer skills, etc.

Employees are people. Ask how they are feeling. If their daughter was sick, ask if she is feeling better. If their father passed away, offer your condolences, and express empathy. Sometimes the support a person needs is not something in the office. Perhaps they could use some help finding a veterinarian because their dog is sick. A typical command and control manager might wonder why anyone would bother to do these things. A true leader cares about people and they understand that their role is to make other lives better. Even the best employees cannot perform at their best if they are struggling with challenges at work or home.

Kelly Brogdon Geyer

Week 12

"Failure is not fatal, but failure to change might be."
Jhn Wooden

Apple is my favorite example of a company that is not afraid of failure. They have had countless products that flopped and I do not foresee that changing anytime soon. The Apple III, Lisa, Newton, Pippin, Power Mac G4 Cube, and others were all Apple products that were disastrous. So how can Apple continue to be the world's largest IT company by revenue despite these failures? Change! They have regular brainstorming sessions with the entire organization and a culture that supports creativity. While brainstorming, they use free association without regard to what is possible or even feasible. Most importantly, everyone knows that if their idea fails, it is okay. Apple fails fast and learns even faster. If one product fails, the next one is likely to be another one of their huge successes like the iPhone or iPod.

Learning from your mistakes and changing is the key. Figure out what went wrong *and* what went right, then adjust accordingly. Eliminate the fear of failure. The key is to keep moving forward.

The world is full of companies that died because of their inability to change with the times. I remember the 1980s and 1990s when I could walk into a video store to rent a funny movie to watch at home. Those stores have disappeared. Remember Polaroid? They failed to recognize changing technology and keep up. Many "brick and mortar" bookstores like Borders closed because they were too late in jumping into the e-reader business or were unable to transition to the new environment of digital and online books. Failure to change could be fatal!

Current success is not a guarantee of future success. Organizations can no longer rely on one product craze to last very long. Even a giant like Apple will die if they launch the next iPhone and then stop innovating. And the change cannot solely focus on products. Companies must constantly evolve to be more efficient, deliver value to customers, improve employee engagement, upgrade technology, etc. When one company fails in any of these areas and does not change, another company will swoop in and make it happen.

Week 13

> *"We may encounter many defeats but we must not be defeated. In fact, it may be necessary to encounter the defeats, so you can know who you are, what you can rise from, how you can still come out of it."*
> *Maya Angelou*

Commitment. Perseverance. Tenacity. Dedication. These are words that come to mind when I read this quote from Maya Angelou. This state of mind must be present before facing any major challenge. Maybe you want to run a marathon, learn to play the guitar, or start your own business. Anything that takes effort and time is likely to experience setbacks.

It fascinates me when I hear of companies who decide to become Agile but then give up after one large project fails or does not happen perfectly. More often than not, the company is relatively new to Agile and the employees have not all embraced the new mindset. They are barely figuring out how to work in teams and have some form of a retrospective. Then a large project is thrown into the mix and everyone has to figure out this new way of working on large projects across teams. There is a key piece missing from the puzzle. Remember that Agile does not mean the absence of processes and planning. It is a common mistake with large scale projects to overlook these components.

So without the new processes in place and before the appropriate level of planning takes place, everyone jumps into the shallow end of the Agile pool headfirst. This is okay. This is one way teams can start to develop new processes for handling large projects. This is one way teams learn to collaborate with other teams. Learn by doing. The trouble arises when tight timelines are enforced on the project rather than selecting the first few large scale projects to experiment with less pressure. Unfortunately, many companies abandon Agile if the project misses a deadline or consumes too much capital. This is an epic symptom of misunderstanding Agile. Think of it in terms of driving a car. If a teenager is learning to drive a perfectly operational car but crashes due to a lack of experience, would you blame the car? Of course not. Would you assume this kid should never drive again? No. They need help learning the rules of the road, how to shift gears, use turn signals, parallel park, etc. That takes patience and practice.

Week 14

> *"In any given moment, we have two options: to step forward into growth or to step back into safety."*
> *Abraham Maslow*

Abraham Harold Maslow was an American psychologist who studied Sigmund Freud but was a bit critical and his approach was quite different. Freud focused much of his research on people with serious psychological issues while Maslow studied mentally healthy individuals who represented optimal psychological health and function. He was best known for creating Maslow's hierarchy of needs. This theory of psychological health predicated on fulfilling innate human needs in priority with the ultimate motive of reaching one's potential. The interpretation of Maslow's theory is represented on the following page in a pyramid with the basic needs at the bottom. He theorized that the most pressing needs would need to be satisfied or mostly satisfied before someone would focus or give their attention to the next highest level need. For instance, a person would not focus on morality or property (safety) if they do not have enough to eat or drink (physiological). At the very top of the pyramid is the need for self-actualization. This occurs when individuals reach a state of harmony and understanding because they are engaged in achieving their full potential.

I often comment on how difficult it is for people to go through an Agile transformation. It is difficult for many reasons. Some people do not like change. Some people become fearful about their jobs. Some managers fear the loss of control. Some of the aspects that are often overlooked pertain to the needs in the pyramid below. When a person has been doing their job for a long time, they become comfortable. They know what to do and how to do it. They can answer most or perhaps all questions. When that changes and they are forced to learn something new, this impacts their need for esteem. They are now being asked to participate in something unfamiliar. They are unsure of the next steps, processes, tools, etc. Their confidence and self-esteem are no longer the same as it was before.

Most organizations struggle during any transformation

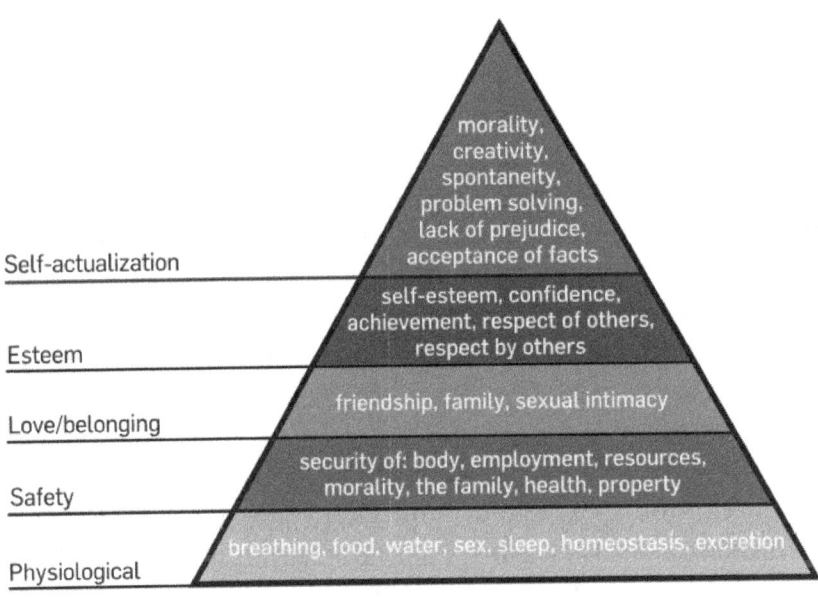

and I suppose they expect employees to perform as if they are in the top level of the pyramid but the employees may be fighting to fulfill their other needs that are lower on the pyramid. Many companies in the US pay their employees a salary that is not a living wage. It is more than minimum wage but not enough to afford an apartment or to pay basic bills like food, heat, and water. How can a person come to work with fresh ideas and ready to solve problems if their stomach is rumbling from hunger or they are worried about their electricity being shut off?

What about companies where there is a lack of job security? Or there is in-fighting and too much office politics? What happens in companies that are reluctant to promote people based on performance and instead promote the person who has simply been there the longest? These things all impact the psychological needs of employees. There cannot be an expectation for people to perform as if they are self-actualized when the organization is not willing to support other basic needs being met.

Assuming the needs on the bottom three sections are being met, I think most companies ignore the esteem needs but expect employees to perform at the next level of self-actualization. For a person to have their esteem needs met, they need to feel comfortable with what they have accomplished. They need to feel competent and recognized. This may entail restructuring the career paths within the company. It may involve having tiered job roles. Perhaps some people require training to push their knowledge to the next level. Sometimes it helps to have dedicated time for positive reinforcement. It requires a change in the way the business operates.

The way people are rewarded and given incentives needs to be examined. The old approach is based on individual performance but that cannot stay the same in a team-oriented environment. New career paths need to be defined. For instance, it might make sense to have a Junior Team Member, Team Member, and Senior Team Member roles. Provide training so people have the ability to progress in these tiers. For employees to feel confident and have positive self-esteem, they need management to support them and tell them when they are doing a great job. When there is a problem, do not point fingers and condemn anyone. Focus on the problem and find a solution together. Preferably, the solution discussion should happen together and be implemented together. The simplest suggestion is to ask employees directly what they need to feel better about their professional lives. But be prepared to actually listen.

To summarize, employees should not be expected to be at the top of the pyramid of self-actualization if their self-esteem and competency needs are not met. If a person does not feel competent in their abilities or they do not feel appreciated, they will most likely not seek opportunities for creativity or become engaged in achieving their full potential. If a company wants employees who are moral, creative, spontaneous, and can solve problems without prejudice, it makes sense to ensure the basic needs are also a focus.

Week 15

> *"It doesn't matter how good you are today; if you're not better next month, you're no longer Agile."*
> Mike Cohn

While it is important to celebrate achievements, it is equally if not more important to inspect, adapt, and improve. Within the Scrum framework, a retrospective occurs at the end of every sprint. Regardless of which framework you use or if you have created your own Agile way of working, it is imperative to build in time regularly for improvements.

Continuous improvement is the 12th principle in the Agile manifesto: At regular intervals, the team reflects on how to become more effective, then tunes and adjusts its behavior accordingly. Schedule these sessions and do not skip them. Generate ideas to try during your next iteration. In the next session, evaluate the effectiveness of those ideas and generate new ideas for the next iteration. When you stop doing this, agility is lost.

Week 16

> *"The secret of change is to focus all of your energy, not on fighting the old, but on building the new."*
> **Socrates**

Change is difficult. This tidbit of information is not a secret. However, some people seem to find it easier than others to adapt. These people can live in the moment and embrace what is happening today, not what already happened yesterday.

Focus all of your energy on building something new. In reality, Agile principles and values have this "focus ahead" mentality built into the philosophy. We need to be responsive to change. Instead of wasting time being upset about something that did not go as planned, we need to concentrate on how to respond to the current situation. Time-boxed reflection time is embedded to think of ways to improve and be more effective in the future. We cannot change the past so it is pointless to dwell on what was, what could have been, or what should have been. Turn your attention to what you want and how to get it.

Week 17

> *"We cannot become what we want to be by remaining what we are."*
> Max De Pree

Think of anything you have ever wanted to change about yourself. Did you want to travel more? You probably needed to save more money and budget more carefully. If you want to be more organized, you probably need to plan better and stop procrastinating.

Transforming an entire organization is even more complicated because it involves more than just one person. Nevertheless, many of the same processes and methods are applicable whether you are an individual trying to change or a large company. It is crucial to determine why the change is wanted or needed and how you want to get there. Figure out what you are willing to change about yourself. More importantly, figure out what you are not willing to change because this will be a true indicator of how much you truly want to transform.

Week 18

"It's not about perfect. It's about effort. And when you bring that effort every single day, that's where transformation happens. That's how change occurs."
Jillian Michaels

Knowing what you want to achieve and having a plan to get there is critical but there is a danger of frustration if you are not perfect from the beginning. This happens frequently with newer Agile teams. They start learning more and more about Agile and what it means. They become frustrated that quality is not perfect immediately. They think they are not Agile "enough" unless they have a certain amount of automated testing. They make significant efforts to become cross-functional and feel defeated if team members are not "T-shaped" after a short period of time.

However, it is worth pointing out that being Agile is not about being perfect. The Agile principles focus on change and regular reflection time to continuously improve. Imperfection is acceptable. To remain static is not.

Week 19

> "...the Agile movement in software is part of a larger movement towards more humane and dynamic workplaces in the 21st century."
> Rowan Bunning

Truly embracing an Agile mindset involves more than simply changing the way projects are managed in an organization. There needs to be a change in the way people are treated.

In a traditional organization, projects are driven by deadlines. If people need to work 50-60 hours per week or more to meet the deadlines, so be it. Although most organizations would claim they focus on quality, one of the first things to suffer when trying to get too much work done in a short amount of time is quality. Schedule estimates are notoriously inaccurate because they are usually done by people who have never done the actual work. If the timeline has not already slipped by the time development starts, it is very common for it to start slipping at that time because duration estimates were not accurate. Everyone is working overtime and still falling behind. People are tired and overworked so small mistakes are being made. Then it is time for testing. At the beginning of the project, it was estimated that testing would take 6 weeks. Unfortunately, all of the milestones that came before were late. Of course, the launch or go-live date cannot move so now testing has to be completed in only 4 weeks instead of the original 6 weeks. Many test cases are omitted and testing is rushed. Everyone on the project continues to feel the stress and work too many hours. By the time the product launches, there are still defects, everyone is exhausted, the blame game begins. Everyone now refers to this as the "Project from Hell!"

However, there is a better and more humane way to work. When we start working in smaller iterations, issues are discovered and corrected more quickly. With autonomous teams, they decide how much they can accomplish in a certain time period. More time and effort are spent collaborating. In a well-functioning Agile organization, employees are not considered resources. They are people. They have families, health issues, hobbies, friends, etc. They cannot and should not be treated like robots that can work endlessly. Before any hard dates are assessed, there should be some discussion with the individuals who will actually perform the work so they have the opportunity to provide input and negotiate.

Furthermore, companies must remain dynamic and flexible. Project dates may be fixed but the scope is not. The goal is to deliver early and continuously. If you give a milestone date, you can almost guarantee it will not happen any sooner than that date. Try to think of it in terms of cleaning your home. If someone told me I have 30 minutes to clean my house, I would get it done in 30 minutes but it would not be very thorough. If someone told me I had 6 hours to clean my house, I would use all 6 hours probably even cleaning things that are not necessary. But if someone told me to clean my whole house but did not give me a time limit, I would most likely get it all done in 3-4 hours. To anyone else coming into the house, it would look just as clean as if I had spent 6 hours scrubbing away. In terms of an organization, it is better to give people the time they need to complete the work rather than the time you *think* they need to complete their work.

Week 20

"Big egos have little ears."
Robert Schuller

In an organization, big egos can have a devastating impact. An egotist is focused on themselves with little concern for others. They possess a sense of superiority and confidence that exceeds their abilities or talent. They believe they know everything and feel that nobody in their immediate circle can teach them anything of importance. They are disconnected from people because they twist the truth to support their ego. An egotist will never admit fault or take responsibility. When something goes wrong, it will always be someone else's fault. What effect does this have on employees and an organization as a whole?

Egotists surround themselves with people who only agree with them even when they are wrong. This leads to poor decision-making and misaligned strategies. They hesitate to make decisions because they cannot be wrong or fail. They underestimate challenges because they do not take the time to fully understand the scope. They might attempt difficult tasks or roles without the skills or ability to do them. Egotists do not care about the needs of anyone other than themselves. They fail to motivate or lead effectively. They will not reflect on personal shortcomings because that would require the egotist to admit they are not perfect. An egotist in a leadership role at an organization can be debilitating and cause losses in productivity and profits.

Week 21

"I know this transformation is painful, but you're not falling apart; you're just falling into something different, with a new capacity to be beautiful."
William C. Hannan

People spend years and even decades trying to get comfortable in their careers. Having change forced upon you can be quite frustrating. However, when you start thinking about a change in a positive way, amazing things can happen. Consider all the breathtaking things that happen in nature due to change. Caterpillars morph into butterflies. In autumn, leaves change from green to stunning shades of red, orange, yellow, and brown. Mountains form when tectonic plates shift. Heck, even several animals change gender during their lifetime! This is survival.

Understandably, change can be scary especially because big changes usually mean the result is unknown. On the other hand, if you think of change as an opportunity rather than a challenge, imagine the possibilities!

Week 22

> *"Leadership is the art of giving people a platform for spreading ideas that work."*
> *Seth Godin*

In my opinion, this concept is one of the most difficult for managers to grasp. However, it also provides an easy tool to determine who is a leader and who is a manager. A manager will see a problem and try to come up with the solution on their own. Or they will come up with their own ideas without much input from others. When they try to implement those ideas or solutions, the result is typically less than stellar. Then they blame the employees who were forced to implement it. A leader recognizes that they do not have all the answers. They know the best solutions and ideas come from more than just one person. Their role is to facilitate those brainstorming sessions, make sure each person has the opportunity to speak, and inspire action.

But how do we know which ideas will actually work? The short answer is that sometimes you do not know until you try. So you need to break down the idea into smaller pieces. Determine the smallest piece of work needed to test out the idea while minimizing the risk. Your role as a leader is not to ensure that nothing ever fails. Your role is to help others have the confidence to express their ideas without fear of failure, visualize success, provide a roadmap of where you want to go, come along on the journey with everyone and learn quickly from mistakes. By consistently doing these things and displaying the tenacity required to be a leader, you will produce a group of people who trust you, believe in you, and will work hard to achieve the shared vision.

Week 23

"The only man who never makes a mistake is the man who never does anything."
Theodore Roosevelt

While experimentation is crucial for innovation, the right culture needs to be in place first. If there has been a history of new ideas being met with fear and rejection in the past, eventually people stop wasting their time talking about new ideas. Start to lead by example by making your experiments visible and transparent. Try new things. Celebrate success *and* challenges. I would go so far as to say to get rid of the words "fail" and "failure." If we learn and adapt when things do not go as planned, the experience can be considered a success rather than a failure. If everything you ever try turns out perfect without any mistakes or missteps, are you really pushing yourself to achieve things or are you taking the safe route to avoid disappointment?

Kelly Brogdon Geyer

Week 24

"Agile teams don't lead to an Agile organization."
Klaus Leopold

Progress is sometimes slowed due to factors outside the team. When one area of a company is Agile (or trying to be Agile) but the rest of the organization still has not adjusted their way of working, frustrations and conflicts arise. Those teams will require their other colleagues to be just as responsive and fast as they are becoming. When teams learn to be more efficient, it will be pointless if they have to wait for Marketing or Legal or Sales to catch up.

The goal should be to have an Agile organization rather than an organization with some Agile teams.

A Year of Agile Quotes

Week 25

"The only lasting form of discipline is self-imposed discipline."
Dale Brown

Discipline is defined as "the practice of training people to obey rules or a code of behavior, using punishment to correct disobedience." Discipline imposed by outside forces is temporary and leads to resistance and rebellion. People show discipline out of fear of punishment and/or to appease the external person imposing the discipline, i.e. spouse, boss, teacher, coach, police, etc. This does not mean the person is truly disciplined. It means they have learned how to *display* discipline. They have learned to make sure the disciplinarian sees what they want them to see.

We see this all the time in the real world and I remember even doing this when I was a child. My mother was very lenient but my father was *very* strict and disciplined us with punishment and fear. My brother and I were incredibly well-behaved when we were with him. We never argued. When my dad asked us to do something, we jumped up and did it. When we spoke, we only used words of respect like, "Yes, ma'am. No, sir. Please. Thank you. God bless you. May I please...?" This did not mean we were well behaved all the time. If he wasn't around, we knew he couldn't see what we did. When we were with our mom, we were little brats. We had all this naughtiness bottled up inside that needed to get out!

This translates into the professional world as well. When employees are micro-managed using command and control, people are not happy. They do not actually do what they are told to do. They simply learn how to avoid getting caught. They have learned how to *display* discipline to their manager to avoid being fired. Discipline imposed by the outside is ineffective in the long run.

On the other hand, self-imposed discipline is long-lasting and empowering. If you are a manager struggling with issues in your department, open the door to discussions. State the issue and ask your team to come up with solutions. Talk through the solutions with them. Have retrospectives to discover new ideas and encourage employees to resolve issues themselves. Most importantly, allow people the freedom to manage *how* they work. Clearly explain *what* you want or expect and then let them determine the best way to do it.

Week 26

"If you adopt only one #agile practice, let it be retrospectives. Everything else will follow."
Woody Zuill

Retrospectives are incredibly underrated, in my opinion. Having dedicated time to reflect and adapt is imperative whether you are using Scrum or Kanban or some different framework.

A retrospective is an effective method of ensuring continuous improvement in a team or a department. Do not use this event as a complaining session. Make sure to discuss what went well and what did not go well. Most importantly, think of a couple of experiments to try or action items for the team to improve.

At the next retro, discuss the results of those experiments or action items to determine if they should be continued, improved, or discontinued. Have retros regularly and, over time, your team will become like a well-oiled machine.

Week 27

> "The more efficient you are at doing the wrong thing, the wronger you become. It is much better to do the right thing wronger than the wrong thing righter. If you do the right thing wrong and correct it, you get better."
> Russell L. Ackoff

This quote by Russell L. Ackoff makes my skin crawl due to the grammar but he makes a valid point. The poor grammar in this quote is certainly not a reflection of his intelligence. Ackoff was an accomplished visionary in the fields of operations research, systems thinking, and management science. He authored or co-authored 35 books including *Redesigning the Future: A Systems Approach to Societal Problems* (Ackoff, Redesigning the Future: A Systems Approach to Societal Problems, 1974) as well as over 150 journal articles.

We need to be cautious about the difference between efficiency and effectiveness. Efficiency pertains to doing things right and effectiveness is about doing the right things. Both are important. Organizations are often tricked into thinking they are on the right track if they are becoming more efficient. However, are they becoming more efficient at doing the wrong things?

I have observed this firsthand in the workplace. A company will pressure their Agile teams to deliver more quickly. Managers make the incorrect assumption that this is categorically a good thing. Unfortunately, if the teams have not managed to address quality properly, they will just deliver poor quality faster. The focus should first be on quality and doing the right things to ensure quality such as investing in training, defining what quality means for the company, building more automated testing, refactoring weak or unstable code, etc. When the right factors are in place, then the focus can shift toward efficiency or doing things right. When you implement the right things, you can turn your attention to doing them faster and better.

Week 28

"Quality comes not from inspection, but from improvement of the production process."
W. Edwards Deming

If your idea of improving quality is to inspect your product after it is made and catch defects before shipping to customers, you are missing the point. Quality assurance does not start after the product is made. Quality should be part of the process during every step of production.

Extensive effort should be made to plan, develop, execute, and automate tests throughout each stage of development. The product should not move to the next step of the process until quality is checked and verified.

A Year of Agile Quotes

Week 29

> *"Never tell people how to do things. Tell them what to do and they will surprise you with their ingenuity."*
> General George S. Patton

Being a groundbreaking leader does not mean you have all the best ideas, everyone does what you say and they do things the way you want. It is essential to cultivate a creative climate where ideas can be openly expressed and discussed without fear of ridicule or reprimand. Brainstorming is a powerful tool for innovation and exchanging ideas that sometimes lead to the next revolutionary invention.

A leader is responsible for providing vision and inspiring people to go there. How that vision is achieved should be open for interpretation. Convey to people *what* you want and let them tell you *how* they will get it done.

This concept is amazing for managers to keep in mind in a slightly different context. It is drilled into your head to "grow your people." Simply enrolling them in training courses should not be the only solution. When an employee comes to you with a problem, the first instinct for many managers is to solve it or ignore it. What if you talk to the employee about ways to solve the issue? The first thing you should ask is, "What have you tried already?"

There are several follow up questions that could help you help your employee arrive at the solution themselves:

- If you were me, what would you do? Do you feel empowered to take that step yourself?

- If you try that, what could be the potential risks and outcomes?
- What can I do to support you in finding a resolution?
- Is there anyone else we should invite to the conversation to discuss ideas?

Week 30

"Be stubborn on vision but flexible on details."
Jeff Bezos

This is similar but slightly different than last week's quote. Think of this in terms of taking a road trip. You have a destination in mind. Perhaps you are headed to Disneyworld with the kids! You wanted to do this the old fashioned way so you mapped out your route before leaving the house. After driving for 30 minutes, you arrive at a detour. The road you planned to use is closed. What do should you do? Would you turn around and go home or find another route?

It is still possible to achieve your vision of spending an amazing vacation at Disneyworld, going on fun rides, enjoying the beach, and taking loads of pictures to share on social media. Taking a different path can still bring you to your destination. It may take a little bit longer but it may actually be faster or have a better view than the one you had planned.

Week 31

> *"The way a team plays as a whole determines its success. You may have the greatest bunch of individual stars in the world, but if they don't play together, the club won't be worth a dime."*
> **Babe Ruth**

    I think this quote is fitting especially considering it comes from a baseball player. Baseball is one of those sports that requires the entire team to play as a cohesive unit. If there is a player who only cares about his own statistics and the team is less important to him, this will hurt the team.

    Imagine his team has the bases loaded and this player is next up to bat. He rarely hits a home run but he knows he could get to first base if he hits the ball to left field. Unfortunately, this means the person on third base may not be able to make it home and score for the team. If he sacrifices himself and hits the ball toward first base, his stats will take a hit but there is a very good chance the person on third base will make it home and score the winning run.

    This scenario makes it very clear how important it is to have teammates who put the team first and make sure everyone understands the goal. The goal is for the team to win the game, not to improve your own statistics.

A Year of Agile Quotes

Week 32

> *"Failure is not the falling down, but the staying down."*
> *Mary Pickford*

The world is full of people who failed but did not give up. Bill Gates started a company that created reports from raw traffic data. It failed. The author of the immensely popular *Harry Potter* series, JK Rowling went through quite a difficult time in her life before the success of her books. She was divorced and on welfare as a single mother. She pitched the manuscript everywhere and was rejected by 12 major publishers before finally having it accepted by Bloomsbury. Walt Disney was fired from the Kansas City Star and his first animation company dissolved because he was unable to pay his rent.

Imagine what our world would be like if these pioneers quit before hitting success. The only reason for their triumph was their willingness to not give up.

Week 33

> *"As a general rule of thumb, when benefits are not quantified at all, assume there aren't any."*
> **Tom DeMarco and Timothy Lister**

    The concise book *Waltzing with Bears: Managing Risk on Software Projects* (DeMarco & Lister, 2013) is full of common sense ideas on how to avoid some well-known pitfalls in software development.

    While refining your backlog and speaking with stakeholders, it is important to know the business value and/or customer value of what your team is working on. If there is no quantifiable benefit, why are you doing it?

Week 34

> *"Success is not final, failure is not fatal; it is the courage to continue that counts."*
> *Winston Churchill*

Achieving success should not be your destination. It is fleeting. Life is incredibly boring if you set a goal, achieve it, and then stop. How do you occupy time? Every effort should be made to put success in your mindset.

Failure is also not fatal. As pointed out in Week 32, many successful people failed miserably before changing the world. Embrace failure as an opportunity for learning and growth.

The courage to continue is what counts. Many people assume that the last part pertains to the failure part of the quote but it applies to success as well. Have the courage to continue after you fail but also have the courage to aim higher once you have achieved what you wanted. Set a new goal and go for it.

Week 35

> *"Rome wasn't built in a day, but they were laying bricks every hour. You don't have to build everything you want today, just lay a brick."*
> James Clear

This James Clear quote frequently comes to my mind during retrospectives. Teams will often have big ideas but they are paralyzed by thinking about implementation. They will voice the idea and then say things like, "But refactoring our entire codebase will take forever" or "Building a new system will take years so we can't do it." People are accustomed to thinking in terms of huge projects rather than small steps.

When this happens, the first thing I ask the team is, "What is the smallest step you can take to check this idea?" Think of the first thing you need to do to verify if this is the right direction? Then take that step. When you complete that step, verify if this is something worth pursuing. Think of the next small step to move forward and so on. By doing this, you reduce risk and enable your team to make quick corrections.

Week 36

"Perfection is not attainable, but if we chase perfection we can catch excellence."
Vince Lombardi

According to Merriam-Webster's Dictionary, something that is perfect is "entirely without fault or defect." I have a very strong opinion about perfection. I think it is pointless. Nothing remains perfect for any significant amount of time. The most beautiful sculpture will degrade over time. An expensive sports car will eventually begin to require repairs. Even the best software in the world will become obsolete or be replaced with something better. Perfection is fleeting and unattainable in the long run.

However, excellence is achievable and honorable. Being excellent doesn't even mean you have to be the best. Think of the Olympic Games. Only one person for each sport will go home with the gold medal. Does that mean that one person is the only excellent athlete? Of course not. The gold medal winner was the best on that day but every athlete who works hard enough to compete in the Olympics is an excellent athlete. Perhaps you could say the winner was perfect on that day. But eventually, someone will come along and break another record. It does not take away from the excellence of the other athletes. That remains. Perfection is fleeting but excellence can stand the test of time.

Week 37

"Intelligence is the ability to adapt to change."
Stephen Hawking

In week 36, there was the idea that perfection does not last. So how can you ensure you stay in business and your product continues to be purchased by consumers? Change.
Industries and companies that fail to pay attention to the constantly evolving environment will die. Nothing is static. The list of things that need to be on the radar is endless: consumer needs, technology, climate, the economy, politics, market trends, etc. Intelligence is a key factor in being able to analyze changes, make predictions, and act quickly to stay in the game.

Week 38

> *"Our greatest weakness lies in giving up. The most certain way to succeed is always to try just one more time."*
> *Thomas A. Edison*

Most of the greatest innovations, inventions, discoveries, and successes in history came after countless failures. Persistence is the defining factor. If there is a truly extraordinary and revolutionary idea, it will never come to fruition if someone is unwilling to fail repeatedly, try again, fail, and try again.

This comes with a caveat. Simply a willingness to fail and try again is not enough. Learning from each failure is essential. Failing is fine but making the same mistake over and over and over again is just stupid.

Week 39

> "Architecture is a bad metaphor. We don't construct our software like a building, we grow it like a garden."
> Craig Larman

Talking about software in terms of architecture absolutely has a bad feeling for me. When a building is constructed, it can stand on its own without much rework for years or even decades. Every so often, it may need to be repainted, get new floors, etc. For the most part, though, it can be left to the enjoyment of its occupants.

Software, on the other hand, will die if it is left alone much like a garden. Anyone who has ever maintained a garden can tell you that it is a lot of work. Gardening is not a "set it and forget it" type of hobby. A good gardener will carefully plan where each fruit, vegetable, or flower will be planted and how each one interacts with the other surrounding plants. He or she will try to determine what kind of weather the coming season will bring. A lot of thought goes into how each crop will be harvested and used. A gardener knows that you have to continuously put work into a garden to be able to continuously reap the benefits.

Week 40

"We ought to be as rigorous as we can with the things we can control."
Dave Nicolette

Life is full of unknowns, uncontrollable factors, mysterious events, and wild moments. It can sometimes feel tumultuous. Nevertheless, there are ways to calm the chaos. Focus on the things you *can* control.

I have never had to do this more than during my wedding planning. I kept my thoughts focused on the goal – getting married to my best friend. I made mental notes of all the things that were outside of my control; family flying in from out of town, weather, someone getting sick, etc. My experience in project management took over and I made detailed plans for everything that needed to be done.

I decided which things would be okay if something bad happened. We had a "candy bar" so everyone could make their own bag of candy to take home as gifts. If the guy didn't show up to put everything together, I was okay with that. No contingency plan was needed. I had a few things that I felt needed a plan B. If the cake did not arrive, we could order something from the hotel at the last minute. If the weather was bad, we had an alternate indoor location for photos. And this is how I planned the entire day.

This may have seemed like overkill but I was able to have a completely stress-free day. My husband and I were able to spend quality time together with our families during the week before the ceremony and really enjoy it without worrying about any of the things that could go wrong. The controllable things were under control.

Week 41

> *"Cooperation is the thorough conviction that nobody can get there unless everybody gets there."*
> Virginia Burden

People sometimes confuse cooperation with an agreement. These are not the same. Cooperation is simply working together with one or more people to accomplish some common goal. This does not require agreement from everyone except for agreeing on what the goal is. Once a common goal is established, there is no doubt that unless all parties involved achieve that goal, nobody will achieve it.

Think of this in terms of a road trip with friends. There are 2 women and 2 men in one car. They are traveling together to celebrate the birthday of another friend who lives quite far away. There might be several challenges along the way. The car will need fuel. The car could break down and need to be repaired. Road construction or an accident on the way might force them to take a different route. They will need to stop to eat along the way. An agreement is not necessary to reach the destination.

For example, imagine it is time for lunch. Three of the passengers want burgers but one passenger wants sushi. The entire group decides to check the maps to see if everyone can get what they want. Unfortunately, the only sushi restaurant is an hour off their route and would cause them to be late for the birthday celebration. The passenger who wanted sushi decides to go where the rest of the group wants to go. They find a place that is just off the highway so they do not need to get off their route. The friend who wanted sushi does not order a burger but finds a chicken sandwich on the menu instead.

In this example, the entire group did not agree on what to eat. They did not need to agree. All of them kept in mind that the goal is to reach their destination in time to celebrate. Everyone was hungry so it was necessary to stop for food. After exploring options for location, it was decided that they needed to find somewhere along their route so they did not waste time. Once the restaurant was located, they did not need to agree on what to eat. Each person could eat what they wanted from the menu. Everyone was happy and they reached their friend's house in time for the birthday festivities.

Week 42

"Never confuse movement with action."
Ernest Hemingway

Movement is anything that causes change. An action is a movement with a purpose. This simple, succinct quote from Ernest Hemingway perfectly captures the essence of frustration in many organizations. Managers try to measure output. How many lines of code were created? What percentage of obsolete code has been deleted? How many stories have you done? How can we increase velocity? How can we increase the number of automated test cases? Unfortunately, these types of measurements do nothing but provide some visually appealing charts. They accomplish very little if anything at all.

Instead, imagine measuring things that matter. How are you measuring value for the customer to ensure you are delivering the high-value items first? What are the overall objectives of the department and what are you working on to contribute toward those objectives? Which items do not contribute to any larger goal and should be abandoned?

Week 43

"We rise by lifting others."
Robert Ingersol

Everyone has heard of the expression, "We are only as strong as our weakest link." Helping other people helps to strengthen the links in the chain. Teamwork is the collaborative effort of a group of people to achieve some common goal.

If there is one team member who works a bit slower than the others, it is advantageous for the rest of the team to help them get up to speed. Otherwise, the team will take longer to reach their common goal. If there is a team member who is not able to work with the level of quality the team wants, it is in their best interest to help them learn how to focus on quality. The consequence, if this is not done, is that the quality of work for the entire team suffers.

Having a team set up in a way where there are some less experienced employees working alongside more experienced employees serves this greater purpose. When someone has been doing a certain job for 10+ years, there is usually a finite amount of improvement that can be observed in their work. However, they cannot complete the work of the team by themselves. They are usually in a team with other people who have far less experience. The overall quality of the work delivered by that team will improve as the skills of the junior members improve.

Week 44

"Failure is simply the opportunity to begin again, this time more intelligently."
Henry Ford

Failing is acceptable. Whenever you try something innovative and new, you can expect to fail numerous times before you succeed. However, continuing to fail at the same thing over and over again without learning from your mistakes is a waste. Start with a theory and then test it. If it fails, blindly trying the same thing again makes no sense. When something fails, determine why. Adjust your theory and test it again. This process of inspecting and adapting is at the core of agility.

Week 45

> *"A leader takes people where they want to go. A great leader takes people where they don't necessarily want to go, but ought to be."*
> *Rosalynn Carter*

This quote by Rosalyn Carter can be the basis of an entire book by itself. Great leadership is required when branching into new markets, expanding skillsets, launching a new product, etc. A delicate balance must exist for people to embrace this type of leadership. If a leader wants to bring people along to a place outside their comfort zone, the key is to start with small steps and a clear goal or mission. It is important to create an environment of psychological safety and the acceptance of failure. Doing this will make people more willing to venture into the unknown.

Week 46

> *"There is nothing so useless as doing efficiently that which should not be done at all."*
> *Peter Drucker*

One of the core ideas of agility is to deliver value to the customer. There should be a constant evaluation of processes, tasks, reporting, and so on to ensure that what is being done is still necessary and useful. In all that you do, ask yourself why you are doing it. What are you gaining? What is the gain for the customer? Who will use this new feature? Is this process still applicable and can we automate it? This bug exists on a page of our site that has no traffic. Do we really need to fix it? If the page has no traffic, do you need the page at all or can you remove it?

By discontinuing unnecessary work, you free up time to be able to focus on the work that matters most so you can do it well.

Week 47

"The only way to go fast is to go well."
Robert C. Martin (Uncle Bob)

There is a common misconception that being Agile means being faster. This is not necessarily the case. People misconstrue the concept of frequent delivery.

Think of it in terms of eating a meal. At the traditional restaurant, you place your order for your meal. You wait for 20 minutes and your food arrives at your table on one plate. It took a little bit of time because the chef had to cook each element for you. That 20 minutes seemed like an eternity because you skipped lunch. You have a delicious salad, steak, potatoes, and carrots.

Now imagine you are at an Agile restaurant. The first dish you order is a side salad. It arrives at your table within 4 minutes. It is delicious. Now you are in the mood for cooked vegetables so you order some potatoes and carrots. They arrive within 9 minutes. You eat half of them and then order a steak with some herb butter to compliment the vegetables. The steak and butter arrive within 7 minutes. Everything is delectable and you finish your meal.

At both restaurants, the meal arrived within 20 minutes. However, at the Agile restaurant, you were able to satisfy your hunger sooner because you could receive the separate parts of the meal as you ordered them and they were ready. You did not have to order everything at once and wait for everything to be ready before you could eat. You were also more satisfied at the Agile restaurant because you could order a side of herb butter to compliment the side dish that you could taste before the steak arrived.

The quality of the food is also better because your salad

was freshly made and brought to you immediately. It did not get warmed up by being on the same plate as the hot food. The chef was able to concentrate on one dish at a time to ensure the flavors were perfect.

Week 48

"Nothing endures but change."
Heraclitus

Few things in life can be more infuriating than trying to fight change. The battle is futile. The cells in our bodies are constantly regenerating. The stars in the sky are burning. Every year, seasons change as spring turns into summer and summer transitions to fall, and so on. Babies do not stay small forever. They change and learn new things. When growth fails to occur, it is an indication that something is wrong.

The secret is to discover ways to embrace change when it comes. Adjustment, transformation, evolution, revolution…it has many names. Call it what you want but change is not something negative. It is not something to be avoided. On the contrary, changes should be embraced as opportunities for growth. Perhaps it is not a coincidence that only one letter is changed to turn *change* into *chance*. A shift in circumstances is a chance for you to experience something new.

Week 49

> *"Adopt the attitude that continuous planning is a good thing – In every iteration, expect your plans to change (albeit in small ways if your planning is effective). Don't fall into the trap of thinking that the plan is infallible."*
> Ian Spence and Kurt Bittner

One of the most misunderstood concepts of Agile that I have seen is the idea that being Agile means you do not plan. Quite the opposite is true, in fact. Planning happens continuously. If you are working in the Scrum framework, you have sprint planning. Within the sprint, you have Daily Scrums where the teams plan the work for the next 24 hours.

One of the most difficult aspects I have seen in organizations is the idea of quarterly or yearly planning. More often than not, it is a colossal waste of time and effort with far too much detail to be useful to anyone. There is typically no valid reason for drilling down details for something that may or not happen a year into the future. What usually makes more sense is to have a high-level forecast for one rolling year. Items that are to be worked on next contain far more detail than the items that will not even be started for 10 months.

If you are working in iterations, the items to be worked on in the next 1-2 iterations should be broken down into enough detail that the entire team knows what to do. These are usually user stories. Items that are three months out on the calendar can be left as features or epics. Items that are six months to one year away can be left as themes with only enough high-level details to give a rough estimate of how long each will take.

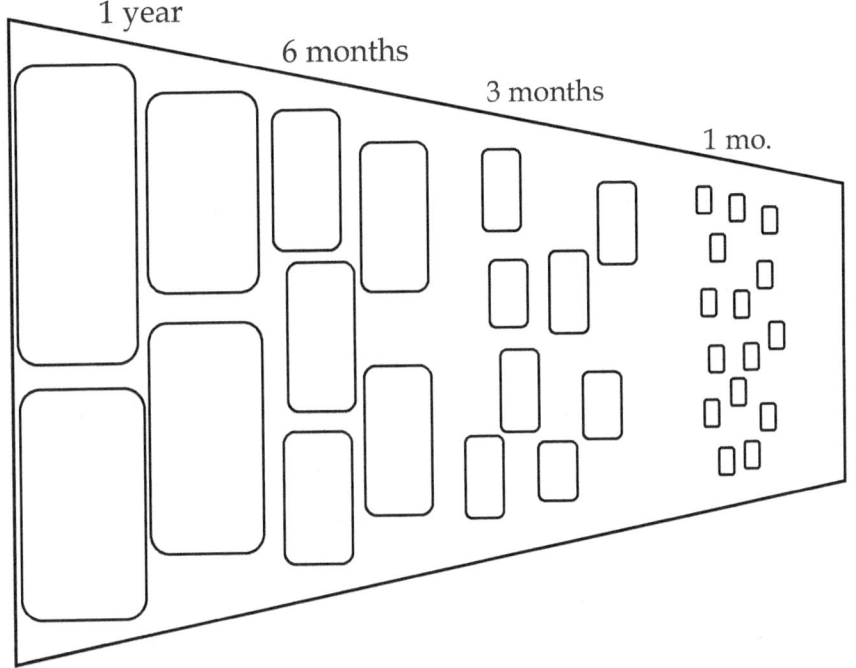

Week 50

> *"The important thing is not your process. The important thing is your process for improving your process."*
> Henrik Kniberg

While there is value in having processes, especially within teams, it is also important to realize that processes should not be static. Process improvement includes identifying, analyzing, and improving processes within an organization, department, team, etc. This task is imperative to optimize performance, meet best practice standards, improve quality, and enhance the user experience.

With Scrum, the task of process improvement is "built in" to the framework in the form of retrospectives. Regardless of how your team is set up, make sure you have a process for improvement. Call it a retrospective or come up with some other name you like. Decide within your team how often and when you will do it. I highly recommend doing it at least monthly and do not skip them.

There is an easy formula for success and there is a myriad of fun ideas to get your creative juices flowing during these discussions. During your process improvement session, talk about the things that have gone well since your last session, what has not gone well, and agree on a few process improvements to experiment with. One key part of this session is to ensure the team actually follows through on their experiments they agreed upon. When I am facilitating, I ask the team members to voluntarily take ownership of the items by writing their name on the sticky note.

The process does not end there. At your next process improvement session, discuss the results of your experiments.

Was there any improvement? Can you think of something else that could improve this process even further? If the experiment was not successful, what did you learn?

Week 51

> *"Simplicity is the ultimate sophistication."*
> *Leonardo da Vinci*

Simplicity is one of the twelve principles of Agile. There is a natural gravitation toward products and services that are simple because they do everything that we need them to do but none of the things we don't. The design and user experience should be as simple as possible.

Years ago, I was shopping for a new stove. I saw one that looked gorgeous. It was sleek, simple, modern, and fit my price range. Unfortunately, it was so futuristic I could not figure out how to use it. The stove was a smooth glass surface without buttons, stickers, lights, or any indication of how to just turn it on. The design was nice but my user experience was negative enough to lead me to purchase a different oven.

Carefully consider each new feature in your backlog. It is crucial to discover what your consumers *actually* want versus what you think they want and what you are capable of. Frequently, new features are added to an existing beloved product only to leave the majority of consumers wondering, "Why on earth did they do this? Who would ever want this?"

Week 52

"Scrum is like your mother-in-law, it points out ALL your faults."
Ken Schwaber

Too often, people assume that Agile or Scrum or Kanban or any other mindset or framework will be the miracle that fixes all the problems. Nothing could be further from the truth. Scrum is not a magic wand that can be waved around to repair issues. Scrum is more like a magnifying glass that zooms in and makes existing issues almost impossible to ignore.

If your organization has cultural issues, you will need to work to fix the situation. If you have weak leadership, Scrum will not create amazing leaders. If you do not have a quality product, you will need to work hard to change that. Working within the Scrum framework will highlight these types of issues and shine a light on them.

References

Ackoff, R. L. (1974). *Redesigning the Future: A Systems Approach to Societal Problems.* New York: Wiley.

Business Dictionary. (2019, January 18). *Definition.* Retrieved from Business Dictionary: http://www.businessdictionary.com/definition/self-organization.html

DeMarco, T., & Lister, T. (2013). *Waltzing with Bears: Managing Risk on Software Projects.* Addison-Wesley.

https://www.merriam-webster.com/dictionary/perfect. (n.d.). Merriam-Webster's Collegiate Dictionary.

Lally, P., Van Jaarsveld, C. H., Potts, H. W., & Wardle, J. (2010). How Are Habits Formed: Modelling habit formation in the real world. *European Journal of Social Psychology*, 998-1009.

TIME. (1966, February 25). THE FUTURISTS: Looking Toward A.D. 2000. *TIME Magazine.*

About the Author

Kelly Lynn Brogdon Geyer has worked in a variety of industries including financial services, construction, health insurance, and telecommunications. She is a certified Project Management Professional (PMP®), Agile Certified Practitioner (ACP®), Certified Scrum Master (CSM®) and holds a Scaled Agile Framework (SAFe®) certification. Her focus is on guiding organizations and teams on the journey to finding better ways of working. She enjoys expanding her own knowledge about various tools, processes, and resources available. Kelly grew up in southern California and then lived in Connecticut for ten years before moving to Austria in 2017. She is married and has two boys.

In her spare time, Kelly enjoys traveling, cooking, crocheting, reading, wine tasting, and Nordic walking.

www.ingramcontent.com/pod-product-compliance
Lightning Source LLC
Chambersburg PA
CBHW070305220526
45465CB00004B/1759